West Dorset, East Devon Walks and Local Attractions

I.S.B.N. O - 907683 - 03 7

NIGEL CLARKE PUBLICATIONS

Tappers Knapp
Tollgate Cottage
Uplyme
Devon
Tel. Lyme Regis 3669

Reprinted 1984
Reprinted 1985

INCLUDES
The Walks

Branscombe .... 2½ hours
Lyme Regis — Seaton .... 4 hours
Lyme Regis — Pinhay Bay .... 2½ hours
Wootton Cross, Coney's Castle, Lamberts Castle 3½ hours
Lyme Regis — Charmouth .... 1 hour
Charmouth — Black Ven .... 1 hour
Charmouth, Catherston, Wootton Fitzpaine ... 2½ hours
Uplyme, Hole Common, Whitty Hill .... 3 hours
Abbotsbury, Chapel Hill .... 2½ hours
Seatown, Langdon Hill, Golden Cap .... 2 hours
Hardy's Monument to Portesham .... 3 hours

Attractions

Fleet Air Arm Museum, Yeovilton
Bicton Gardens
Barney's Fossil Collection & Country Life Museum
Cricket St. Thomas
Seaton Tramway
Philpott Museum, Lyme Regis
Exeter Maritime Museum
Perry's Cider Farm
Bovington Tank Museum
Wookey Hole, Wells

FOREWORD

I was going to dedicate this book to Spooks, the family dog, who seemed to think that writing books about walks was the best idea since the invention of 'Bonio', but I'm afraid while he enjoyed the walks he thought the writing part dull though he willingly accepted his royalty rate in biscuits!

The walks described in this booklet are all in the West Dorset and East Devon area covering up to Abbotsbury in the east to Branscombe in the west. The lengths of the walks are all no more than a morning or afternoon. Where beach walks are mentioned (Lyme Regis to Charmouth) please check the times of the tides. One drawback to walking in Dorset and Devon, especially for members of the 'Flat Earth Society' are the hills all seem steeper than the last, but the views from the top are a just reward and at least you will return fitter..........I hope!

Many of the footpaths are extremely boggy and rutted so I would recommend a stout pair of walking shoes, wellington boots are a disaster for walking distances in even if the path is very muddy I would still wear hiking boots.

Some of the coastal sections of the walks are very exposed and high winds while exhilerating at first soon become a misery so such walks are best left to calmer days.

An ordnance survey map is a necessity especially on inland walks where footpaths are hard to follow and often cut by barbed wire fences a compass is also a good idea. All footpaths are open to the public and are legally rights of way. If a footpath has been blocked by barbed wire or some other such obstruction then it is a criminal offence, though please understand some of the farmers problems of trampled crops and dog attacked livestock especially during the lambing season.

Always shut gates and avoid walking over crops and keep any dog on a lead when crossing fields with livestock in.

I hope at a later date to expand this booklet so any ideas on favourite walks or suggestions would be most welcome. I would also like to thank The National Trust, The Heritage Coast, local councils and the many other groups and bodies with out whom our unique system of footpaths would not exist.

Nigel J. Clarke May '82'

The Viaduct ~ Uplyme

BRANSCOMBE   3¾ miles (2½ hours) walking moderate.

This historic and attractive village nestles into the most westerly outcrop of England's chalk cliffs. Sidmouth is 3½ miles to the west and Seaton 3 miles to the east. Take the Branscombe turn off from the A3052 (Lyme Regis to Exeter road). The lane is narrow and twisting, follow the sign for the beach, and park the car in the park to the front of the beach restaurant. The footpath starts at the back of the restaurant, go up the hill and through the gate towards the former coastguard cottages. Dogs should be kept on a lead while crossing the first two fields as they frequently contain sheep and lambs in spring. Follow the footpath across the second field and cross the stile onto the wind swept expanse of west cliff. Behind and to the left in the valley is the village of Branscombe, nestling and hiding from the sea and protected from winter gales. Hooken Cliffs are opposite the scene of a major landslide in 1790, when 10 acres of land slipped and plunged 200ft into the sea. The coastline here is subject to continuous erosion and 3 metres is lost on average each century. The footpath continues in a westerly direction along the easily followed cart track, though on a hot summers day it is nicer to benefit from the sea breeze nearer the cliff edge. The track runs through the lightly wooded hills and is heavily rutted and muddy after rain. The local woodland contains a variety of flowers including daffodils, bluebells, red campion and scabious, more pungent is the aromatic smell of wild garlic. The track passes a new plantation on the side of the hill. Follow the footpath until a gate is visible obstructing the path 30 metres ahead, then follow the footpath sharp to the right, though not easily distinguished. There is scrub on the left and an open field on the right, eventually reaching Pit Coppice on the right then skirting round the woods until reaching a stile. The path after the stile descends through the woods to the small village of Branscombe, with its picturesque thatched cottages and well maintained gardens. The footpath emerges at the side of Rookeries Cottage.

Turn right and follow the road towards the sea and car park. On route you will pass the blacksmiths forge still working and used, there is also a bakers which uses faggots of wood

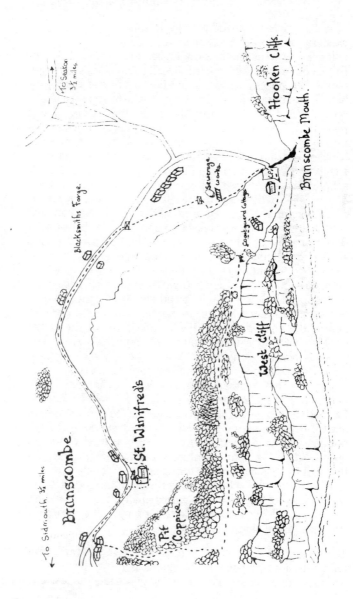

To Sidmouth. 3½ miles

Branscombe.

St. Winifreds

Pit Coppice.

Blacksmiths Forge.

To Seaton 3½ miles

Sewage Works

Coastguard Cottages

West Cliff

Hooken Cliffs.

Branscombe Mouth.

to bake the bread. The route also passes the parish church of St. Winifred's, this attractive stone built church features a tower and nave built in 1140 during the Norman period, though the original site is believed to date much earlier than this, as a church is known to have existed there in Saxon times. The chancel of the church, built in the 14th century, has a wagon roof made from over 60 metres of oak beams, there is also an interesting three tier pulpit in the church. The house opposite is 13th century and was the former curates home, though now a private residence.

Follow the road until reaching a footpath that crosses two fields and you will eventually be back at the car park.

The Cliff Walk from LYME REGIS to SEATON.
(Time 3½-4 hours) Walking hard, 6 miles.

The walk starts from Holmbush car park, which is located at the top of the town on the Seaton road. The path onto the cliffs is in the right-hand corner of the car park and is marked by a sign outlining the route of the Southwest coastal walk of which this walk is part. The track goes past the houses and onto the start of Ware Cliffs. The footpath runs parallel to the sea and to the left of the old town reservoir of which only the earth embankments remain.

A delightful view of the Cobb below, it was from these cliffs during the English Civil War that the Royalist forces fired on the Parliamentary held cobb, sinking several ships. Also from Ware Cliffs can be seen Stonebarrow and Golden Cap, and on a clear day Portland Bill.

Follow the footpath up towards the bungalow, which nestles into the cliffs, pass through the gate and turn left onto the cart track that leads down to Underhill Farm. To the right of the track is the start of the heavily wooded nature reserve. At Underhill Farm the footpath begins. The start of the path is marked by a conveniently placed sign and map of the route. Underhill Farm was one of several local locations used in the filming of the French Lieutenant's Woman, the cinamatic adaptation of John Fowles locally based novel.

The first section of the path can be extremely boggy, especially after heavy rain, boots and a stout stick are a necessity at such times. In spring the sides of the footpath are scattered with wild primroses and later, bluebells. In the late summer the gorse and bracken are easily ignited so care should be taken with matches and cigarettes. One of my favourite spots of the walk is soon reached. A large, heavily shaded pond that seems to attract an abundance of birds, heard only when you the walker is silent. It's surprising how much noise we tend to create when walking, and how completely oblivious we are to the animal and birdlife around us. It is worth pausing by these ponds to listen in quietness, you will be surprised by the number of bird sounds and if you are very lucky you may even hear or see some of the larger animals that live in the reserve such as deer, fox and badgers, though such animals are more easily seen on dawn walks.

After the ponds the footpath passes some old ivy clad walls, long since fallen into ruin. The walls were built by a local land owner in the last century to keep trespassers out, though in his enthusiasm to preserve his privacy he also blocked off a public right of way but after a prolonged series of legal battles people were once more allowed to use the footpath.

Much of the land in this stretch of the walk is moving and slipping towards the sea and it is dangerous to wander off the path, especially to the sea-side. The footpath eventually emerges onto a rough track, built by the Water Board for the maintenance of their pumping station at Pinhay Bay. The walking is easier and less muddy than the previous section of footpath. The track eventually reaches the green painted pumphouse of the Water Board, and a convenient turn round point for those either too tired or through lack of time to carry on to Seaton.

Beach walk back to LYME from PINHAY PUMP STATION (Tide Permitting) Turn left down the path onto the beach following the water outfall pipes. The path is particularly muddy for the last few yards before reaching the beach. Make sure that the tide is a good way out before turning left

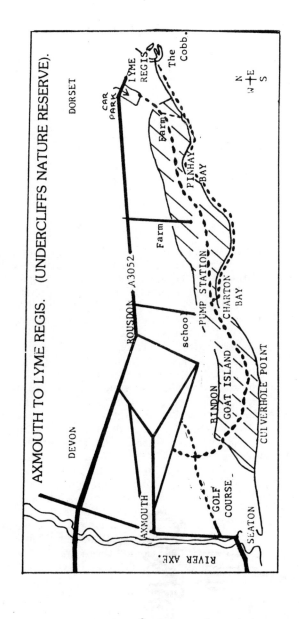

AXMOUTH TO LYME REGIS. (UNDERCLIFFS NATURE RESERVE).

and walking back to Lyme. (Even better have a tide timetable). The walk along the beach takes just over the hour but stay well clear of the cliff-face because of falling rocks and debris.

PINHAY PUMP STATION to SEATON

The cliff top track is well sign posted and runs up the hill to the side of the pump station and then turns left running parallel to the sea and towards the west. A short walk beyond the pump station, the force of earth movement has pulled the roots of large trees out of the ground, tilting the land nearly 2ft over a 12 month period, the footpath has also been disturbed, but I congratulate the people who regularly maintain the path and build new steps as required.

Depending on the time of year, a pungent smell permeates through the air, have no fear you are not about to stumble on a remote part of the Wimpy Empire, the plant responsible is the wild garlic that grows in profussion all along the side of this stretch of the path. The footpath carries on up and down, though the up's seem to come quicker than the down's, eventually reaching a clearing and spring at Charton Bay. The water has been channelled into a series of pools, an ideal place to wash muddy shoes and children, the pools contain much frogspawn and later in the year tadpoles. In the surrounding vegetation you will find adders and grass snakes, though the adder is found in greater numbers and some large specimens have been found in recent years, but are such shy and timid creatures that few are seen by walkers. The footpath carries across the bridge (the track on the right goes on up to Allhallows School and eventually out on to the main road at Rousdon) and turns off to the left, then to the right at the second intersection of paths. Slowly the path ascends, eventually reaching Bindon Cliffs, the scene of the most spectacular slip in 1839. The slip occurred shortly before Christmas of that year after an exceptionally wet autumn. Fifteen acres of farm land (as it was then) slipped down into a chasm and remained in tact with hedges and growing corn fields. The pressure of the slip uplifted a reef a quarter of a mile off shore, 40ft high and nearly a mile in length. The slip attracted much publicity though little of the resulting chasm can now be seen and the reef has long since been destroyed by the sea. There is a picture of the ship in the Harbour Inn at Axmouth, (a refreshing stop to eat and drink after the walk) which was drawn at the time.

The footpath ascends the cliffs and eventually comes out on to the farmed downlands, typical of Dorset and Devon's sheep farming. You cross the stile and follow the path along the field. In the second field, cross diagonally to the gate in the far corner and follow the hedge on the left of the gate onto the farm track. At the end of the track is the golf course walk straight onto the golf club and following the tarmac road down to the river.

═══════════

WOOTTON CROSS - CONEY'S CASTLE - LAMBERTS CASTLE. 3½ hours, Walking easy.

Wootton Cross is on the B3165 on the Hunter's Lodge Crewkerne road. If you are crossing from Bridport or Lyme Regis take the main Axminster road until reaching the junction at Hunter's Lodge Public House. At the junction take the B3165 for Crewkerne. Wootton Cross is some 3 miles from the junction. The easiest way to know when you reach Wootton Cross is that shortly before the cross roads the road is straddled by large power lines hanging from meccano christmas trees. After the sign post for Fishponds there is a lay-by which is the most convenient place to leave the car. The start of the footpath is a brief stroll back to the cross-roads, on the left 10 yards down the road for Fishponds is a gate. The footpath leads off from the gate and through the first field. On the left the path runs diagonally across the field towards the woods. Though the footpath on the ordnance survey would seem to be in the boundary of the fields it will save a lot of scrambling over locked and barbed-wire gates if you cross into the woods and skirt the edge.

After approximately 600 yards the woods open onto a field, the footpath swings to the right of the copse to the side of the field and through the gate out onto a cart track. At the track, turn right past the large house and down the hill. Near the bottom of the track is Nettlemore Farm, the name proudly and conveniently displayed from a gate to the left. The footpath carries on through the gate and down across the two fields where in the right-hand corner is a stile out onto the road. Follow the road to the right, down hill for 200 yards untill reaching a gate on the left.

Across the valley, straight ahead is Coney's Castle, distinguished by its wooded summit. Up the valley to the left is Lamberts Castle. Why two hill forts so close together I can't imagine, perhaps two brothers quarrelled, or ancient Britons just liked building forts. Who knows! Below Lambert's Castle and straddled by a cobweb of power lines is the pleasant village of Fishponds.

The footpath and our route crosses the valley and climbs up owards 'Higher Combe Farm'; the middle cluster of farm buildings facing across the valley. Straight ahead and down the field is the footbridge across the stream, to the left is a recently dug duck pond. From the bottom of the valley looking up one realises the excellent siting of Coney's Castle. The soldier, puffing and panting would have made an easy target for the stone throwing Britons even before reaching the first defensive mound or wooden fortifications.

After crossing the foot bridge walk up towards 'Higher Combe Farm', which is now no more than a few delapidated outbuildings; left over from nineteenth century agriculture. The track runs to the left of the buildings onto the cart track which we will follow to the left towards Lambert's Castle. (A short diversion up the hill are the mounds and remains of Coney's Castle, though little evidence can be seen of this once impressive fort).

The farm track is very boggy and churned by the farm machinery, though easy to follow and emerges after half a mile out onto the road at the delightfully named 'Peters Gore', perhaps named after an early Dorset metador.

At 'Peters Gore' the footpath to Lambert's Castle is well sign posted and for a change the landlord (The National Trust) encourages walkers. After closing the gate, to keep the sheep in and cars out follow the track up the hill past

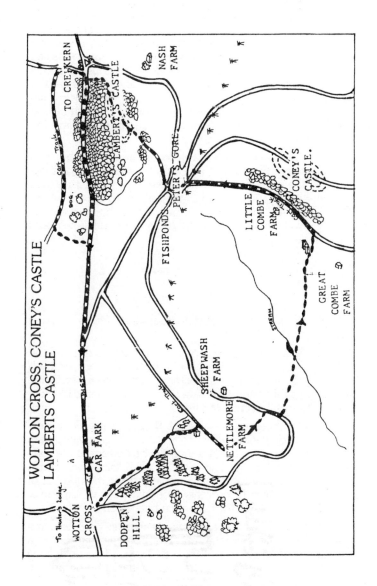

WOTTON CROSS, CONEY'S CASTLE
LAMBERTS CASTLE

To Hunter's Lodge.

WOTTON
CROSS

A 3165

CAR PARK

DODPEN
HILL.

NETTLEMORE
FARM

SHEEPWASH
FARM

FISHPONDS

PETER'S GORE

STREAM

LITTLE
COMBE
FARM

GREAT
COMBE
FARM

CONEY'S
CASTLE.

TO CREWKERN

Cart Track

BOG.

LAMBERT'S CASTLE

NASH
FARM

a newly constructed 'object' which looks like a neo-nuclear fall out shelter, carefully constructed not to blend with the scenery like a wart on Miss World. One advantage of this building is that the earth works make an excellent viewing platform for a visual sweep across the stunningly beautiful Marshwood Vale, from the hills near Dorchester to the sea at Charmouth. The path carries on and as usual up hill towards Lambert's Castle. The bumps and ditches are the remains of Lambert's Castle path. Enter the fort through the old main gate, though now only two overgrown banks. The footpath leaves the castle to the left and runs down the side of the hill to the road.

The walk is at an end and the easiest route back to the car is to follow the road to the left for a mile until reaching the lay-by. For the more adventurous route back follow the track straight ahead and bear off at the bottom to the left where there is another path, though be warned the path here is nearly always boggy and wellingtons or good hiking boots are needed.

LYME REGIS CHARMOUTH beach walk. 1 hour, walking easy.

This walk can only be completed if the tide is out and the state of the tides should be checked. Follow the Charmouth road out of Lyme Regis turning right after the traffic lights, walking up the road to the side of the white painted block of flats. The road eventually drops onto the beach.

After crossing a series of groins that jut onto the ledges, the cliffs rise up looking like multi-layered cake. The layers were once the sea floor, the nearer the bottom of the cliffs the older the period. The rock is called 'Blue Lias' and is particularly important to paleontologists for the number of fossils it contains. It is on this section of cliffs that many of Lyme Regis's famous fossils have been found.

The Blue Liasic cliffs gradually sink away as one nears the cascading cliffs of Black Ven. The frontage marked by a snout of rock mud and debri. These cliffs are almost living and move and fall with such frequency that 2 photographs in

CLIFF AND BEACH WALK FROM CHARMOUTH TO LYME REGIS

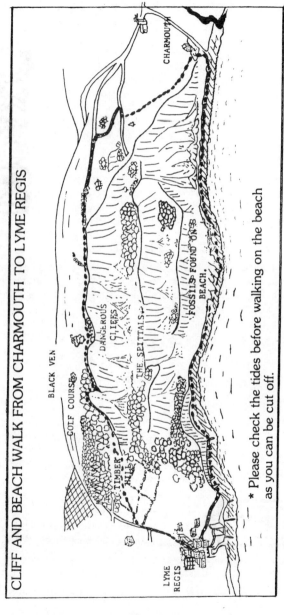

CHARMOUTH

BLACK VEN

GOLF COURSE

DANGEROUS CLIFFS

THE SPITTALS

TIMBER HILL

FOSSILS FOUND ON BEACH.

LYME REGIS

* Please check the tides before walking on the beach as you can be cut off.

a decade would hardly look the same. The plateau up above the beach is treacherous with bog and marsh ready to trap anyone. The cliffs are unclimbable as the face gives way at the slightest touch.

The beach on a quiet day has a variety of sea birds including most of the gull family and groups of oyster catchers. The rock pools contain shrimps and prawns. Offshore are the marker bouys for crab and lobster pots. This beach is reckoned by local anglers to be the best for fishing, as on a high tide, at night, dogfish, skate and conger come in to feed on the muddy beach.

Along the beach is clearly visable the old Charmouth cement works, which is now a cafe in the holiday season. The beach at Charmouth is not without its history. Vikings landed here twice, raping, pillaging and other Viking activities, and there is record of a battle in the area. This was also scene of an unsuccessful escape attempt by Charles II after his defeat at the battle of Worcester.

The car park is the end of the walk, you can now return to Lyme over the cliffs or walk back along the beach (check tide). There is an infrequent bus service that runs through the village of Charmouth.

CHARMOUTH, BLACK VEN, LYME REGIS
1 hour, walking hard.

Leave the car at Charmouth Beach car park. The footpath to Lyme Regis starts at the side of the old cement factory, which in the summer is used as a cafe. As you ascend the edge of the cliffs, to the right are houses and on the left, a view across towards Lyme Regis.

Follow the path upwards, it eventually comes out onto a road, take the lane straight ahead, at the end of the lane which is 150 yards long is a junction, turn left up the gravel road, this road peters out at the start of the golf course.

You will be pleased to learn that you have now covered the hardest part of the walk and have ascended over 400 feet.

A short rest and a look at the view show how worthwhile this initial climb has been, behind are the valleys and hills of west Dorset. A look along the eastern coast shows the magnificence of Stonebarrow and Golden Cap, and near the end of the coast before the land hooks round to Portland Bill, is the famous Chesil Beach. Lyme Regis lies below to the west, the Cobb protectively snaking out to sea, usually on the horizon to the west of the harbour are giant oil tankers and cargo vessels which favour the sheltered waters of Lyme Bay as an anchoring spot.

The footpath follows the edge of the cliffs towards Lyme Regis skirting the edge of the golf course. Below the cliff is a sunken plateau area known as the Spittals, a dangerous boggy area, rich in plant and animal life. In early evening and at dawn, rabbits, foxes and badgers can be observed moving about this geological sanctuary from the cliffs above. The area also provides a rich habitat for grass snakes and adders, though they tend to keep clear of this well trodden footpath. The footpath leaves the golf course, disappearing to the left of the fence and eventually channelled by a hedge to the right, gorse and bush to the left, this section of the path is often muddy. At the end of the path is a sign erected by the National Trust, take the left path; marked 'Coastal Path Lyme', which winds its way down the hill through deciduous woodland which is known as Timber Hill. At the bottom of the wood you come out onto the Old Lyme Regis, Charmouth Road. This former Roman road once ran along what was then the top of the cliffs, but was abandoned in 1924 due to the movement of the terrain which swept part of the road away.

Turn left along 'Old Lyme Road' for about 10 yards and take the path on the right which crosses down the fields towards Lyme. This area is owned by the Dorset National Trust and the fields have many varieties of wild flowers and plants which were once common, though are less frequently now seen on commercially farmed land.

The path runs down across the fields towards Lyme, and comes out onto the main road opposite the cemetery. Follow the road down hill into the town. Just opposite the car park on the left is a magnificent eighteenth century mansion, though now, alas, has fallen into a severe state of disrepair, despite having a conservation order on it. The road into town also passes the Parish Church of St. Michaels, the present building dating from sixteenth century, though there is evidence of an earlier Norman structure of which only the nave survives.

You now have a choice, the main part of the town is just round the corner though if you wish to set back for Charmouth along the beach, take the road to the left past the Parish Church. There is a sign on the corner for Wiscombes the builders! This road leads down to the beach, though watch the tides.

CHARMOUTH, CATHERSTON AND WOOTTON FITZPAINE. 2½ hours, walking easy.

The walk starts from the centre of Charmouth High Street. Which is easy to find as there is only one main road. The lane at the start of the walk runs to the side of the bankers by the traffic lights. Barr's Lane comes out onto the town playing fields. This well worn path crosses the fields down towards a tributary of the river Char. There is a bridge in the second field to save a soaking. After the bridge, the walk is up hill towards Catherston Manor. The footpath emerges through a gate onto a road opposite the drive way to the Parish Church of St. Mary's. Two large ornate stone pillars guard the access but sadly the wrought iron gates have long since disappeared.

Our track runs across the fields to the right of the Church, due north and uphill. In the next field after crossing the gate the path has been ploughed up, so in order to save trampling crops follow the hedges until reaching a gate on the opposite (northern) boundary. At last we come out onto an easily followed cart track turn right and follow the track round the back of Catherston Manor. The track follows a ridgeway from Catherston towards the pine wooded Conegar Hill ('450') which can be seen to the north east. The walk along the ridgeway offers a view of the surrounding landscape. To the east of the village of Whitchurch Canonicorum, it's most

Charmouth, Catherston, Wootton Fitzpaine.

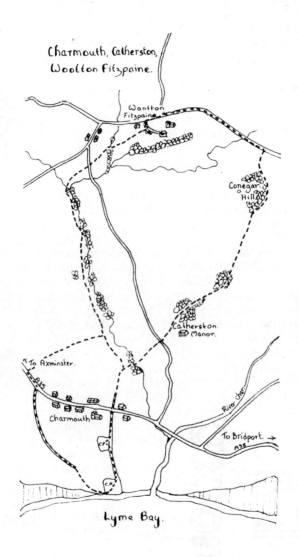

interesting. The church dates back to the Norman period though there are features of an earlier Saxon church which was thought to have existed on the site. The church is also unique in that it is a rare example of a church containing the shrine of its patron saint 'St Candida'. The shrine dates from the thirteenth century.

The other village to be seen from the ridge way is Wootton Fitzpaine, its splendid manor house facing across the valley. In the north is the wooded hill of Coney's castle, an ancient hill fort which rises to 730 ft and is thought to be the site of the battle between the native Saxons and marouding Danes in 833 A.D. King Egbert, a Saxon chieften, defeating the Danes.

The footpath enters Conegar Woods to the right, and a well trodden track runs through the woods and out onto a field. Keep to the right of the field and walk round until a path leads down onto the road. At the road turn left and walk towards Wootton Fitzpaine. A cemetery marks the eastern approach to the village. Near the centre is the old cattle pound, well preserved and looks as if it is still used. To follow the footpath after Wootton Fitzpaine becomes confusing being badly signposted. The path runs to the left off the drive way to Wootton Manor and through the hedge. The drive has a large white gate across it and there is a bungalow on the right and the house lodge on the left. After passing the gate in the hedge, follow the iron fence across the field towards the second turnstile. In the next field take the first gate on the left and there is a footbridge across the stream, half way down the field on the right. Walk across the field towards the road and exit through the gate. The footpath continues across the road and over the turnstile into the next field, if you keep to the hedge then bear left at the gate this will lead you down to the river. From here on follow the river down back to Charmouth.

UPLYME

TAPPERS KNAPP, SLEECH WOOD, HOLE COMMON, WHITTY HILL. 2½ - 3 hours, walking moderate.

The walk is off the usual hikers routes, so in areas the path may be hard to follow. I would advise taking an ordnance survey map.

The starting point of the walk is off the Uplyme road coming from Lyme Regis. Follow the road out of Lyme Regis and take the second turning on the right after the Black Dog Public House. The road you have turned down is Tappers Knapp. Follow the lane down and over the bridge. The walk starts at the unmade road to the right after the bridge. Follow the road past the picturesque thatched cottage called Honeysuckle. After the cottage the path narrows winding its way through woodland. The river Lim is on the right, though hard to see in summer when obscured by overhanging trees. The path passes through a gate onto a green with an old water mill tucked in the corner to the left. The mill is on the borders of Devon and Dorset and was commercially run until the First World War.

The route we will follow is to the left of the mill, over the turnstile and round the back of the house and up and along the old cart track. On the right is Sleechwood which is all that remains of a much larger forest that used to cover this area. The woods are best seen in autumn when they are ablaze with reds, browns and golds. The cart track comes out onto a metalled road, bear right and follow the road up the hill, take the unmade road on the right after the house. The track almost sweeps back on itself. This section of path after rain can be very boggy. The track banked by hedges then passes through a corner of Sleech Wood. The exit from the woods to the fields is blocked by a wired gate, though one is entitled to cross the field using the footpath. After crossing two fields, at the second turnstile turn right, go down the valley where there is a bridge that crosses the stream. Though the footpath is not clearly visible the route carries on up the hill towards Rhode Barton Farm. Leave the fields via the gate to the left of the house. The next section can be the most waterlogged of all. The footpath turns left down the hill and (in wet weather so does a stream)

21

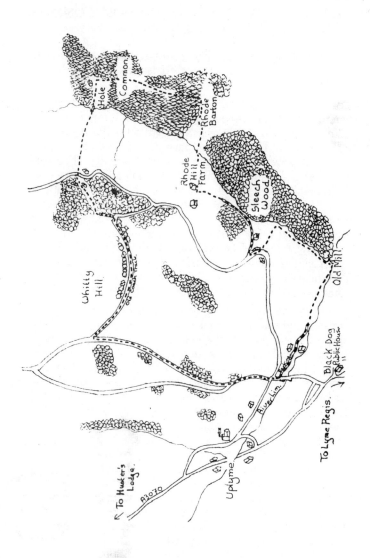

Hole

Common

Rhode Barton

Rhode Hill Farm

Sleech Wood

Whitty Hill

Old Mill

Old Mill

Black Dog Public House

River Lim

To Hunter's Lodge.

A3070

Uplyme

To Lyme Regis.

22

into the woods of 'Hole Common'. Most of the woodland is coniferous plantations laid out in neat rows, the path runs between a tree lined avenue. The plantation is left after passing a small dilapidated wooden barn. A bridge crosses the stream and the path runs up hill to the side of the hedge and comes out onto a road. After climbing over the gate, turn right up the road and take first on the left. The path starts to climb up the side of Whitty Hill, passing through mixed woodland and to the front of an isolated cottage. The path then tracks horizontally up the side of wooded hill towards a gate which opens out into a field. Across the field and to the left is another gate then a short stretch of footpath which opens onto an old cart track. The track runs to the west (right). The view from the hill is panoramic. To the south is Lyme Regis partly hidden from view and in the southwest is the railway viaduct built in 1904 and closed in 1962. The viaduct is said to be the second highest in England, the central pillar being over 90′ in height. The old railway line that runs across linked Lyme Regis to Axminster, but in the sixties became a casualty of railway economic cuts.

Follow the cart track round the side of the hill until reaching a road at the junction turn left and after a twenty minute stroll you will be back where you started.

Water Mill — Uplyme, Devon.

ABBOTSBURY, CHAPEL HILL 2-3 hours, walking easy.

Abbotsbury is one of the most attractive villages in Dorset. Situated 9 miles from Weymouth and 9 miles from Bridport on the B3157.

The starting point for the walk is from a car park on the western approach to the village by Chesil Beach past the Tropical Gardens. It is here that engines are switched off and feet replace wheels!

Follow the track along side the beach to the east until reaching a stile, cross this and follow the footpath along the edge of the field. Straight ahead is a prominent hill with St. Catherines Church built on its top. Our walk basically goes around this hill. Follow the footpath by the fence and cross over another stile and continue along the cart track. St. Catherines Church should be on your right. The track is rutted and care should be taken not to twist an ankle. Our route bears off to the left shortly before reaching a group of farm cottages and a cricket pitch.

The footpath up to the church is through the gate after the stone built barn on the right. The steep climb is well worth the effort. St. Catherines Church was built in the 15th century and is a prominent local landmark for seamen. The terrace on the eastern side of Church Hill are thought to date from Saxon period. The church over the centuries was allowed to fall into disrepair and was not renovated until 1907. The Ministry of the Environment now maintains the building. The view of Abbotsbury from Church Hill is splendid, to the east are the remains of the old monastry and to the the right is the large tithe barn built in 1329. To the west on the hill are the old ramparts of Abbotsbury Castle an Iron Age fort.

Follow the footpath back down the hill from Saint Catherines and take the path to the right round the side of the hill towards the sea. At the small stone bridge crossing the stream keep to the right-hand path. (For those wishing to see the Swannery carry straight on across the bridge and over a stone stile onto the road leading past an old mill, down to the entrance of the reserve). Our path curves round the front of Church Hill. The Swannery is on the left to the east end of the fleet. The Chesil Bank is very

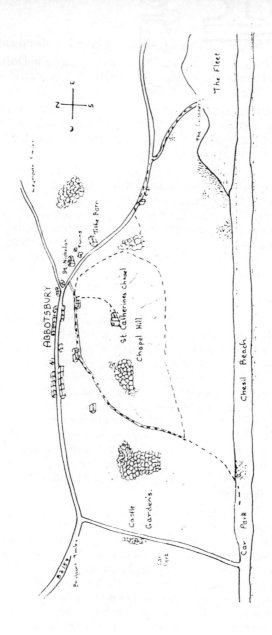

ABBOTSBURY

The Fleet

Chesil Beach

Car Park

Castle Gardens.

Car Park

St Catherines chapel

Chapel Hill

St Nicholas

Ruins

Tithe Barn

Seymour's mews

B3/57

Bridport 9 miles

N E S W

26

prominent. The footpath runs across a couple of fields though is hard to follow. The barbed wire makes crossing an obstacle race, whoever invented the stuff should be shot! Eventually the path reaches the track leading back to the car park at the foot path of the Chesil Beach.

Some history of the buildings on route.

Saint Nicholas's Church.

Saint Nicholas's Church is the main Parish Church of Abbotsbury. The Church dates from the Norman period though was substantially rebuilt in the 16th century. In the church yard opposite the north porch are two stone coffins made from local purbeck marble. On the slabs are two carved figures of what are thought to be two of the early Abbotts of the monastery for which the Church was primarily built. The old manor house is opposite the Church.

The Ruined Abbey

Abbotsbury was an important ecclesiastical centre though little now remains of its once important Abbey. The Abbey was founded in 1026 by 'Orc' the steward of King Canute and dedicated to St. Peter. The monks were from the strict Benedectine Order. After the reformation the Abbey passed into the ownership of the Strangeway family who later became the Duke of Ilchester. During the Civil War much of the Abbey buildings were destroyed. The large pond to the left of the ruins was once the main fish pond where carp were bred for the table. The most complete building from the monastic period is the great Tithe barn, now part of Abbey Farm. The building is the largest medieval barn still standing in the country. From its size and capacity one can guage the importance of the monastery.

The Swannery

Though now a nature reserve the original function of the Swannery was to provide swans for eating and was founded by the monks from the monastry. The swans are attracted to the Swannery by the cleaner drinking water as those on the fleet are too brackish. The Swannery also attract many other water fowl. The reserve is open to the public from mid-may to mid-september.

The Tropical Gardens

The gardens were founded by Elizabeth the First, Countess of Ilchester and were originally the gardens to her summer residence which burnt down in 1914. The gardens survive and contain a unique collection of rare species and sub-tropical plants.

─────────────

SEATOWN, LANGDON HILL AND GOLDEN CAP. 1½ - 2 hours, walking hard.

Seatown is a small fishing hamlet on the Dorset coast midway between Charmouth and Bridport. To reach Seatown turn off the A35 at Chideock. Seatown is a mile down the winding, country lane. There is a car park opposite the Anchor Inn Public House.

The footpath to Golden Cap is well marked and runs to the left of the pub up past the former coastguards' cottages, built during a period when smuggling was the second occupation of the fishermen. The path is worn and easy to follow, there are fields on the right and cliff and scrub to the left which offer some slight protection from the wind.

Shortly, there is a sign for Langdon Hill, which is the wooded hill to the right of Golden Cap. Our path crosses the stile and up the side of the field to Langdon Hill. To the front of the woods is a second stile and the track that leads off to the top of Golden Cap. The final climb to the summit is sharp and steep and will have even the fittest puffing and panting, but it is all worth while for you have now conquered the highest cliff on the south coast of England and from now on its all down hill!

Golden Cap is 617 ft above sea level, the highest coastal cliff on the south coast of England. The name is an apt description of the cliff face, the exposed upper greensand and gualt on the summit to the seaward side produces the characteristic golds and yellows of the Cap. The Golden Cap estate is now owned by the National Trust and covers

View of Golden Cap from Charmouth

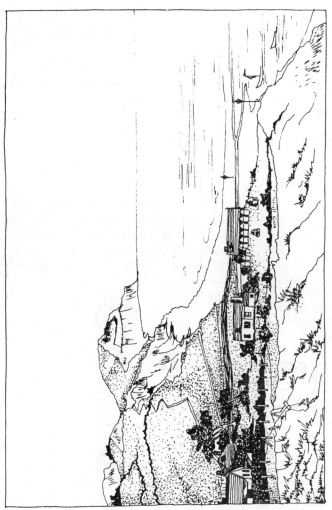

1,294 acres. From the summit are some of the best views of west Dorset. To the north is the little village of Morcombelake, exposed and windswept in winter by westerly winds. To the north east is the forested Langdon Hill. To the west is Charmouth, once the scene of a battle between waring Danish raiders and resident Saxons. Black Ven separates Lyme from Charmouth and is the most unstable of all the local cliffs, no two pictures taken in a decade would look the same as the cliffs continually slip and move.

To the east is the snout of Portland Bill, the hard rock protruding out into Lyme Bay a home to the navy, prisoners and fishermen. At night you can see the light house flashing its warning to passing ships.

A brief excursion down the western side of Golden Cap will take you past the ruins of St. Gabriel's Church. Once the parish church for the lost village of Stanton St. Gabriel. The old coaching road once ran along the coast through Stanton St. Gabriel and on towards Charmouth. Stanton St. Gabriel drew most of its wealth from passing traffic on the coaching route. When a new road was built, due to the old route falling into the sea, it was one and a half miles further inland. The population of Stanton St. Gabriel declined and the village died. The church was built in the thirteenth century and is first mentioned in an ordnance from the Bishop of Salisbury in 1240 at the time it being an important church. By the middle ages both the village and its importance had declined and the parish was administrated from Whitchurch Canonicorum. By the end of the eighteenth century the church was no longer used and became derelict. Enterprising fishermen soon found a new use for the church, smuggling. Brandy, silks and tobacco brought from France were rowed ashore on the quiet deserted beaches of St. Gabriel's and stored in the ruins of the church. Ghost stories were spread to deter even the most persistant of revenue men from investigating the strange flashing lights. The smuggled goods were then taken in-land along the back roads of the Marshwood Vale. Smuggling was largely brought to a halt by the stiffer penalties introduced and the building of coastguard cottages at Seatown. After our brief look at the ruined

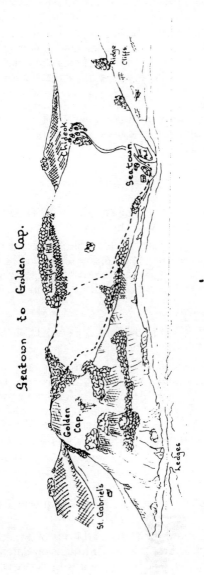

Seatown to Golden Cap.

St. Gabriel's

Golden Cap.

Langdon Hill

Chideok

Seatown

Ridge

Cliffs

Ledges

31

church of St. Gabriel's we return up to the top of Golden Cap. The route back down to the car park is by following the coastal footpath route down to Seatown.

Seatown has always been a small fishing hamlet though increasingly now — caters for the tourist industry with caravans and tents. In former times the chief occupation was netting mackerel from the large shoals that come inshore during the summer. Though with over fishing the large shoals in the last 20 years they have disappeared, though Seatown is still very popular with the beach angler and good catches of bass, conger and cod have been taken from its beaches.

WET DAYS, AND LOCAL ATTRACTIONS IN WEST DORSET AND EAST DEVON.

Even the most ardent walker takes a few days off either through blisters or most common the weather, when it is cold, wet and windy, I have included some of the local houses, museums and attractions with-in the local area.

FLEET AIR ARM MUSEUM, YEOVILTON, SOMERSET (off the A303 near Ilchester).

One of the southwest's premier attractions.

Early aircraft and photographs the history of the Royal Naval Air Service. Among the aircraft on display are a Seafire, a Buccaneer jet, Sea Hawk and the Fairey Swordfish also a number of helicopters. The second ever built Concorde is on display and housed in its own hanger.

Yeovilton is not only a museum but a working Naval Air Station and on any day you may see helicopters, and Harrier Jump Jets taking off.

BICTON GARDENS. On the A376 between Exmouth and Sidmouth (1 April - 31 Oct).

The gardens are the former grounds of a medieval house which burnt down, the present mansion dates from 1730. The gardens were laid out by Andre Le Notre who was chief gardener to Louis XIV of France. He was responsible for the splendid gardens of Verseilles. Apart from the horticultural attractions there is a childrens' play area and a museum of transport with vintage cars and motorcycles.

BARNEY'S FOSSIL COLLECTION AND COUNTRY LIFE MUSEUM. The Street, Charmouth.

Barney is a local Charmouth man and over the years has found numerous fossils on the beaches of Charmouth and Lyme Regis, so keeping the tradition of Mary Anning alive. His unique collection is housed in a museum at the lower end of Charmouth High Street. There is also a collection of country life featuring a blacksmith forge, barn engines and old farm wagons. Barney's is open from Easter to September 10 a.m. - 5 p.m.

CRICKET ST. THOMAS. On the A30 between Chard and Crewkerne.

Cricket St. Thomas is one of the most professionally run parks in the area catering for all tastes. The estate is set in a beautiful Somerset valley with attractive gardens and lakes. At Cricket St. Thomas there is a lot to do and see. The Heavy Horse Centre is particularly good but there is also a delightful tropical aviary. Other attractions include a farm and country museum and a butterfly breeding unit. The estate is open throughout the year in summer from 10 a.m. — 6 p.m. and in winter from 10 a.m. — dusk.

SEATON TRAMWAY TERMINUS, HARBOUR ROAD, SEATON, DEVON.

The narrow guage tramway runs from the car park in Seaton along the river Axe to Colyton. While Seaton itself is not very inspiring the river is most attractive, especially at low tide when the mud flat attracts numerous birds to feed. Colyton is a delightful Devon village and well worth a stroll round. The term cars are open-topped so a good view can be had. The first village you pass after leaving Seaton is Axmouth, in Roman and Saxon times a large port but with the silting up of the river its former grandeur is hidden. The tramway is open from 1 May — 1 October.

PHILPOTT MUSEUM, LYME REGIS.

I always seem to end up in museums to escape the rain

though for the Philpott Museum I would make an exception and even use a dry day. The museum has something to attract everyone from Lyme, lace to an old fire engine. There is also an important fossil collection, all gathered locally. The museum also illustrates Lyme's turbulent history from the seige of the Civil War when Lyme remained for Parliament when all around were falling to the Royalist flag, to the landing of the Duke of Monmouth in his ill-fated mission to take the English throne from James I. The museum is open from 10.30 a.m. — 5 p.m, and at 30p entrance extremely good value. Open from Easter till September.

EXETER MARITIME MUSEUM. The Quay, Exeter. (Free parking)

The museum has a collection of boats from all over the world from a Chinese junk to ocean going rowing boats, there is even an Arabian Dhow. There are in all, over 100 boats and all are open to the public with few barriers or restraints which makes the museum ideal for children. The museum is open all the year round from 10 a.m. - 5 p.m. The museum also organises special events in the summer months though for further information telephone Exeter 58075.

PERRY'S CIDER FARM, DOWLISH WAKE, NEAR ILMINSTER, SOMERSET.

Perhaps more of an interest to adults who would like to see how the west country's most potent drink is made, though the actual mill is only in operation during the autumn months. A thatched barn contains a collection of old and interesting farm implements and wagons.

BOVINGTON TANK MUSEUM. off A352 near Wool.

The Museum has the largest collection of tanks and armoured personel carriers in the country from the Great War II, German Panzers and Tiger Tanks. There are also British early experimental tanks as well as Churchill and Sherman Tanks and many others. There are also displays of uniforms, weapons and armaments. On one tank here there is an outside control stick which drives the turret. Children can clamber over the metal monsters freely as there is little chance of damage. The museum is also situated in the confines of the camp of the armoured Corps so you may be lucky to see modern day tanks on manouvers. The museum is open all year. 10 a.m. — 12.30 p.m. 2 p.m. - 4.45 p.m.

WOOKEY HOLE 2 miles from Wells, Somerset.

A bit further afield but worth the drive are the famous caves of Wookey Hole. The caves carved from the rock by force of water have had many occupants from Sabre Toothed Tigers in prehistoric times to early man. At the time there was even a hermit living in them. There are guided tours of the caves where at least you might learn the difference between stalactites and stalagmites. There is also a fairground collection and Madam Tussauds wax works store room. Wookey Hole is open all year. Near-by is the historic Cathedral of Wells.

FROM HARDY'S MONUMENT TO PORTESHAM. 3¼ miles.

A dominant feature of the west Dorset coast is the Hardy Monument. Many people think that the memorial was built to commemorate the works of Thomas Hardy the author. Alas, they are wrong. The tower was erected in 1844 in memory of Admiral Sir Thomas Masterman Hardy, who was captain of Nelson's flagship at the battle of Trafalgar (The Victory).

We will start our walk from the car park at the monument. To reach the tower take the Bridport to Dorchester road (A35) and turn off at the sign for Martinstown in Winterbourne Abbas. From here the way to the monument is sign posted. There is ample car parking space at the foot of the monument, where some of the finest views of West Dorset can be seen.

The walk
There is a track to the right hand side of the carpark that goes down the hill. Follow this path till it forks and take the fork till you come to a T-junction. Take the right sided footpath and follow the track that curves gently to the right and rejoins the road. Shortly before the road is another track that runs down hill on the left. Take this track passing

through a gate and into some woods. At the bottom of the hill another track joins our footpath from the left and shortly the path divides into three, take the middle path and carry on down hill through the trees. You then pass through another gate and turn right at the T-junction and follow the footpath to another gate set in a wall. Pass through the gate onto a grass track which leads up hill. To your left should now be a fence. At the top of the slope follow the right hand track, through a gateway and along towards and through a second gateway. Our path then curves the outskirts of a field towards a gate in the bottom righthand corner. After this gate the track is gravel covered and leads onto the road into the village of Portesham.

In Portesham follow the road towards the public house (The Half Moon), and then turn left into Winter lane, this leads up hill and out of the village. Follow the road till you come to a cattle grid on your left, where you should pass through the gate and follow the footpath up towards Portesham Farm, which you pass to the right. After the farm another track joins our route from the right. Ignore this footpath and carry on ahead. Pass through another gate and down hill towards Black Down Barn. Shortly before the barn is another gate which you pass through, take the right hand fork, where the footpath divides and carry on up hill till you come to the top of the slope where our route is crossed by another footpath, at this junction turn right. To your left should be a plantation of fir trees while to the right open fields. Carry on ahead towards a large Dutch Barn where you turn left back up towards Hardy's Monument, which can now be seen.

The Village of Portesham

Portesham is one of the least spoilt villages in Dorset. The church of grey stone is interesting, it has a twelfth-century nave wall, a Norman font and a Jacobean pulpit. Not far from the church is the Old Manor House, which is a splendid example of an eighteenth century farmhouse.

Admiral Hardy's former home is situated at the bottom of the main street and is called Portesham House.